SHRUNK

S. E. McKenzie

DEDICATION

To everyone who has been left out in the cold.

TABLE OF CONTENTS

SHRUNK

I

As the world was shrinking
I saw you holding on;
You held on to me too

Without thinking.

Then you brought me down;
I thought I would drown;
In a feeling

That should never be felt on the floor.
The links were so tight
It hurt more than ever before

That night; shrinking value
While some hide in space;
Shrinking privacy;

All over the place
While the Watchers
Stood on corners in the divided city;

One side was pretty
And the other side had
Dead end streets galore;

The Watchers craved blood and nothing more.
Traffic moved too fast
Until it stopped at its regular choking point.

There was just too much smoke
From the fire
And not enough water to put it out.

The Watchers were standing about;
Obsessed with their standing power,
They did not move.

There were broken lines
Interrupted by a shout;
Broken lines;

So many wanted out;
But the Watchers were standing about,
Standing over broken lines,

FLIGHT

That could not sustain life;

Observations fading
Never to be seen again
In the same way.

II

Alienation;
Social Degradation;
Lack of entry point

For integration.
Alienation;
Isolation.

The Watchers
Did not share the same values
With the watched.

Alienation;
A hurt sensation
Behind the Red Line.

III

Who could she have been,
If there were less people blocking,
When opportunities were knocking?

He took his ring off
And hid it
In his pocket.

That way
He could take what he could;
And still demand more.

In the Negative Zone
Alienation
Kept most

Behind the Red Line
While the Watchers
Obsessed with their standing power

Remained standing,
Steely faced,
At their post.

FLIGHT

The bravest from the Negative Zone
Dared to roam
Around the pretty side of town

Before the glare grew too hot to handle.

Then the bravest
Were not brave any more
They went back home

And hid behind their door;
For evermore.
The Red Line

Grew to be their comfort zone;
Where they now belonged;
Where they could be left alone;

Slowly dying within;
This alienation
Was the third sin.

While the Watchers stood;

All in a row
On a skid;
The youth just hid;

Forgetting about tomorrow.

IV

The Watchers were standing at every door;
So obsessed with their power while standing,
They did nothing more;

While the fire raged;
The Watchers saw nothing at all;
Drank into the night

As they did many times before.
They looked in the mirror
Before they left the Fancy Inn.

They felt pride for they were so well-dressed;

FLIGHT

They tumbled with the dispossessed,
Leaving them in their aftermath;
Made the Watchers laugh.

The Timocracy had just begun;
The Watchers made the dispossessed run;
While they remained

Obsessed with standing
Door to door.
Not knowing that this was their first sin;

Violating relationships between neighbors.
Acted as they were from above;
Forgot about brotherly love.

The Watchers were standing about
On the pretty side of town;
Without planning time to reflect.

Riches were not maintained,
As they were all standing about;
Watching those from the poor side of town.

Walking about.
Timocracy;
Descendants of an aristocracy;

Now nothing more
Than a bumbling
Bureaucracy.

Riches suffered from neglect,
While the Watchers drank
The public's money away.

The Watchers didn't know any other way;
All they did
Was watch their day fade away

Into a new night

Again; the Watchers ran out of the door
Leaving the Fancy Inn behind
One more time again.

The ghetto was soon in plain view;
That is how they picked Rose;
And kicked her down

FLIGHT

Past the Red Line on the other side of town.

But Rose had died before;
Beside me
On the floor;

So Rose arose; not really living;
Not yet ready to die;
She was in such pain; it made me cry.

Rose was blamed for her failure;
The Watchers success;
They could afford to be well dressed;

Though they never thought of anything new
To do
Or say;

They were Watchers everyday

Standing around watching
As the time went by;
They jumped to conclusions;

But never found solutions.

The Watchers' staring oppressed
And froze many into fear;
Soon many became dispossessed;

More money went out
While the Watchers were standing about
And the producers were too few

To bring money in;
The Watchers watched
While many were liquidated

Even those who were well to do
And not even hated
The cost of living had inflated

The cost to live was now understated.

And Big Brother yelled out his order
To close the border;
For the only growth industry

Pretty city had
Was Fear of Disorder;
And nothing more.

FLIGHT

The fence went up;
The cup
Was now half empty

There was less cause for envy.

Big Brother said he knew what was best;
Bulldozed what he called slums;
Classified the residents bums.

And on the other side
Of the street; past the lights
The people there were called citizens;

And they were so well dressed

Would fight all night
With the dispossessed.
So they could fill up their cup;

"Put your wall up,"
Another Big Brother said.
"And keep it up

So those outsiders can't get in."
As Jealousy became the second sin;
They said all they wanted to do was win;

Still haunted by their first sin.
They pray to the eye in sky
That had broken down.

It was just a machine

Needed an artificial source
Of fuel to move; it needed artificial energy
To groove.

The eye in the sky
Was Big Brother's
Recorder.

Situated
High above;
So Big Brother could watch the border;

The only growth industry
Was Fear
Of Disorder;

Dividing our world so alive;

FLIGHT

We did what we did to survive;
While Electricity was flashing
Above our world of organic matter;

So fragile
And so easy
To tatter.

In a world that was made for life
The Watchers hid in the shadows
Complaining about what they saw

On the other side of the lights;
After a few beers
The Watchers would let loose

All their fears
Into the Negative Zone
Where the poorest of the poor were walking alone.

The city was divided
In two
By Force; same Power

That divided the Earth from the sky and sea;
Sky that seemed to go on
For eternity;

The Nouveau Colony;

Where mysteries were abounding;
The beauty was astounding.
Silently; hearts were pounding;

In these times of war.

Earth's greatest wealth
Was in her people
Made from True Love

Standing in line for bread;
Slept on the street;
They had no bed.

Yes this was the time;
For the Timocrats to rule;
It was a system that was very cruel;

FLIGHT

Designed by the simple minded;
Hate
Was their bait;

Hate opened Hell's gate;
And it was rumored that the Zombie race
Had taken over;

Fear and Hate
Closed minds;
Hate was now in control of Fate.

Timocrats made problems
That they could never resolve;
Timocrats allowed decency to dissolve

We were waiting until the Timocrats could evolve?
The only growth industry
Was the Fear of Disorder.

While the Watchers
Grew more obsessed
With standing at every door.

Waiting for Zombies
To come out
Of the floor.

While the Zombie economy
Dominated
More than ever before.

To us it felt like a police state
Without due process needed
The Watchers would oppress while they greeted

Us; for the only growth industry left
Was the Fear of Disorder
And nothing more.

Many in the Negative Zone
Struggled to stay afloat;
While the Watchers looked remote and stared

At the dispossessed while taking note;
Waiting for another vote;
All they knew was learned by rote;

As they stood on the Pretty Side of the street;

FLIGHT

Those who owned the land
Were the only ones
To give command

So they
Made it forbidden;
For those from the poor side of town

To be seen
On the pretty side of town.
They were called eye sores

For evermore.

The Watchers made it so;
Followed those
They did not know, including Rose.

They turned around so quick
It made Rose feel sick;
Now they accused Rose

Of following them.

The Watchers needed Rose to fit
Their billing code
So they could get paid

While channeling
Tax money from the poorest part of town
To make the other side of town

Even more pretty;
While they sent Rose to the Shrink
Hired by the Watchers' boss;

Who wrote in Rose's new file with red ink;

Dissolved her identity;
She could no longer be
Who she used to be;

She couldn't even think.

Rose changed, almost over night
And would never be free.
She was now too broken inside

Victim of the self-fulfilling prophecy;

And labelled for life
While the Watchers looked at Rose
As if she were a Zombie coming out of the floor.

FLIGHT

Rose wilted
And faded away
To become nothing more.

The Watchers now watched Rose's every move
So they could build a case against her
Fitting her into their billing code.

Her sense of worth
Would be diminished
For evermore.

Rose would lose her sense of self;
Transferred into Watchers' wealth;
She was now shrunk;

Often put into cells

Of solitary;
The gain for the Watchers was purely monetary.
As she screamed out in Psychic Pain

No one came;
No one knew her at all;
For Rose there was no gain.

Alienation;
A hurt sensation
Haunting the Timocrat Nation.

It was just another day;
The Watchers were authorized
To watch Rose every day;

The pain for Rose
Never went away;
Living under this new way;

For the only growth industry
In the Pretty City
Was fear of Social Disorder;

And Rose was too young to hide her heart.

Alienation;
The Watchers win;
Power corrupts the soul;

This was the fourth sin.

FLIGHT

The Watchers classified
Rose to be insane
As they watched her rolling

In Psychic Pain.
The Watchers picked Rose
To use in their social experiment;

Rose's pain hung from her Psyche;
Felt like cement;
Rose's pain brought her down;

It hurt so bad;
She would rather drown
In Eternity where she could be free

For evermore.

No; it was too soon
To let go; Rose could not fade away;
The Watchers told Rose to repent

And to bow down to the One Percent.

The Watchers watched
While taking notes;
Now Rose would never be the same again.

The Watchers were pleased
With the work they had done.
Now they could shun

Rose; speaking about her
But never to her;
For evermore.

Rose was now processed into the Billing Code;
The Watchers self-prophesied;
One day Rose would explode.

V

Success was measured in Quantity;
Not in Quality.
The Watchers knew who voted for who;

Sometimes names were put on a list;
If they did not vote
For the well to do.

FLIGHT

Fear ruled; while the able were able to flee;
The empty spaces
Gave new opportunity

For the Timocrat Nation
So many lost in Alienation;
Still found Love

To be the best sensation;
Able to lift them beyond
The Red Line on the ground;

Love helped them fly
To new heights;
Never reached before;

When stuck behind
The Red Line
Dividing Pretty City

Part of Timocrat Nation;

Only growth industry
Was the Fear of Disorder;
Gave the Watchers so much opportunity

To watch
Without ever
Having to see.

VI

The police were militarized;
They pierced the youth
With their eyes.

Timocrats wasted youth's time
While they were being paid
By the hour;

The Watchers
Forced youth
To explain their presence

Everyday
Until they either ran away
Or stayed hidden behind the red line.

FLIGHT

VII
Pete
Loved Rose
And came to visit

When he was allowed.
Pete too was lost in the crowd
Behind the Red Line.

Sometimes
Pete
Would share

The little he had to eat.

One day
Pete saw Rose
Hooked up

To a machine without a heart;
Soon the frustration
Tore them apart.

VIII

Lies needed no evidence.
For there was no evidence
To give.

Names were listed so casually;
As people not yet dispossessed
Begged for privacy;

We were all told to shop locally
But when we left
The part of town

Behind the Red Line
We felt put down
As the micro-managers

Asked for our life story
Before they let us
In their door

That was watched by Watchers
More intensely
Than ever before.

FLIGHT

We felt degraded;
The hurt lingered
For evermore.

Watchers took notes
As they stood by the door
Steely faced;

They never spoke;
They grunted
While counting votes;

As the ragged people
Returned books to the library.
They were watched by the police gone military

No longer civil in their duty; they shouted the order
For the only growth industry
Was Fear of Disorder.

IX

Tell me why
Some get ahead
While putting others down?

Tell me why.

X

Hear the Fear
Of Public Disorder
The only growth industry

In the town; was fenced in by a wall;
The xenophobes controlled it all;
Outsiders were not welcomed anymore;

The town was toxic;
The youth felt sick
With fear.

For the militarized police were always near.

Youth needed love to grow
But the atmosphere of Fear
Kept them stunted;

Fear had taken hold;
Many felt hunted;
A strip mall replaced the community hall;

FLIGHT

Where everything of value was sold
Before it turned to rust
And faded away.

While the old feared the young
Big Brothers' rule
Had just begun.

It stayed that way
Until the Youth
Grew Old.

Big Brother did not speak;
And everything you said would be used
Against you the following week.

This was how the Watchers got ahead;
Even though such a Timocracy
Was costly; some also said

A travesty of justice;
For Fear
Grew in the collective head.

The able were able to flee;
Spaces of opportunity were now free;
For the Watchers who were only able

To watch and take notes;
Demanded votes;
Learned by reciting rotes.

The young; the ones not missing;
Stopped believing in Love;
So they were never get caught kissing

Under the apple tree
Of Forbidden Knowledge;
They had lost their courage.

The Timocrats
Worshiped their mechanical eye in the sky
While never doubting the rules

Of their Timocratic world.

THE END

Produced by S.E. McKenzie Productions
First Print Edition October 2015

Enquiries: 1(778)992-2453
Mailing Address:
S. E. McKenzie Productions
168 B 5th St.
Courtenay, BC
V9N 1J4

Email Address:
messidartha@aol.com

http://www.amazon.com/SarahMcKenzie/e/B00H9RWX48

www.ingramcontent.com/pod-product-compliance
Lightning Source LLC
Chambersburg PA
CBHW060546030426
42337CB00021B/4456